A MESSAGE TO PARENTS

It is of vital importance for parents to read good books to young children in order to aid the child's psychological and intellectual development. At the same time as stimulating the child's imagination and awareness of his environment, it creates a positive relationship between parent and child. The child will gradually increase his basic vocabulary and will soon be able to read books alone.

Brown Watson has published this series of books with these aims in mind. By collecting this inexpensive library, parent and child are provided with hours of pleasurable and profitable reading.

Christmas
Songs, Carols and Verses

Text by Maureen Spurgeon
Illustrated by Peter Wilks

Brown Watson
ENGLAND

JINGLE BELLS

Dashing through the snow
In a one horse open sleigh,
O'er the fields we go,
Laughing all the way;
Bells on bob-tail ring,
Making spirits bright,

JINGLE BELLS

What fun it is to ride and sing
A sleighing song tonight!
Jingle bells! Jingle bells!
Jingle all the way!
Oh, what fun it is to ride
In a one horse open sleigh!

SILENT NIGHT! HOLY NIGHT!

Silent night! Holy night!
All is calm, all is bright;
Round yon Virgin Mother and Child,
Holy Infant so tender and mild:
Sleep in heavenly peace,
Sleep in heavenly peace.

MY SNOWMAN FRIEND

I call him Mr. Frosty-Face!
He brings us so much fun,
He has coal eyes, a carrot nose
And a smile for everyone!

When I talk, I know he'll listen
To every word I say,
I can shout, or knock his hat off,
And he'll never run away!

But, when the weather's warmer,
Then Frosty-Face must go –
Until the next time that he comes
With winter's ice and snow.

GOOD KING WENCESLAS

Good King Wenceslas looked out,
On the feast of Stephen,
When the snow lay round about,
Deep, and crisp, and even:

Brightly shone the moon that night,
Though the frost was cruel,
When a poor man came in sight,
Gath'ring winter fuel.

POOR OLD SANTA

We've put up the decorations
With plenty of holly to see,
We've helped Mummy to make
Mince pies and a cake,
We've got the star for our tree!

POOR OLD SANTA

We've hung our Christmas stockings,
But the chimney we did not clean!
Now, there's soot, dirt and mess,
Santa's stuck there unless . . .
He can wait 'til the chimney
sweep's been!

AWAY IN A MANGER

Away in a manger,
No crib for a bed,
The little Lord Jesus
Laid down His sweet head;

The stars in the bright sky
Look down where He lay,
The little Lord Jesus
Asleep on the hay.

SANTA'S SLEIGH

Have you ever wondered
Where Santa leaves his sleigh,
When he brings toys for children
To find on Christmas Day?

For reindeers, all the roof-tops
Are much too smooth and steep!
One slip, they'd go sliding down,
And land in one big heap!

But if they were in the garden,
How could Santa, with his sack,
Climb right up to the roof-top,
Then down the chimney stack?

There's so much danger in the road,
So, where CAN he leave his sleigh?
Perhaps you'd like to ask him,
When he comes round your way!

WE WISH YOU
A MERRY CHRISTMAS

We wish you a Merry Christmas,
We wish you a Merry Christmas,
We wish you a Merry Christmas
And a Happy New Year!

O CHRISTMAS TREE!

O Christmas Tree! O Christmas Tree!
Thy leaves are so unchanging:
Not only green when summer's here
But also when 'tis cold and drear.
O Christmas Tree! O Christmas Tree!
Thy leaves are so unchanging.

THE CHRISTMAS FAIRY

I am the Christmas fairy –
And everything I see,
With wand and crown,
As I look down
From the top branch of the tree!

I see the pretty coloured lights,
The cards hung on the wall,
Candies and sweets,
And Christmas-time treats
For visitors, when they call.

What fun on Christmas morning!
I'll remember all I saw,
When I'm put away
Until the day
I'm on the tree, once more.

O LITTLE TOWN OF BETHLEHEM

O little town of Bethlehem,
How still we see thee lie;
Above thy deep and dreamless sleep
The silent stars go by.

Yet in thy dark streets shineth
The everlasting Light;
The hopes and fears of all the years
Are met in thee tonight.

GUESS WHO!

F is for the Fur trim
     round his big boots and hat,
A is for his Apple cheeks,
     so cuddly, round and fat!
T is for the Toys he brings, and
H his Happy smile!
E is for his Eyes, so bright, and –
R each Reindeer mile!

C is for the Chimney stack, and
H the Hearth below.
R for his Red cloak and hood,
I the Ice and snow!
S is for the Stockings,
T is for the Tree – and
M is for the Mistletoe,
   which we all love to see!
A is for the Angels,
   who on Christmas cards appear
S for dear old Santa Claus,
   who visits us each year!

CHRISTMAS IS COMING

Christmas is coming,
The goose is getting fat,
Please put a penny
In the old man's hat,
If you haven't got a penny,
A ha'penny will do;
If you haven't got a ha'penny,
Then God bless you!